For my niece, Hazel. *H.W.*

First published in Great Britain 2023 by Red Shed,
part of Farshore

An imprint of HarperCollins*Publishers*
1 London Bridge Street
London SE1 9GF
www.farshore.co.uk

HarperCollins*Publishers*
Macken House, 39/40 Mayor Street Upper, Dublin 1
D01 C9W8

Text and illustrations copyright © HarperCollins*Publishers* 2023
ISBN 978 0 0085 2438 8
Printed in the UK by Bell and Bain Ltd, Glasgow.
001

Consultancy by Dr Miquela Walsh, DEdPsych, MsC (Dist),
BSc (Hons), HCPC accredited.

A CIP catalogue record for this book is available from the British Library.

All rights reserved. No part of this publication may be reproduced, stored
in a retrieval system, or transmitted, in any form or by any means, electronic,
mechanical, photocopying, recording or otherwise, without the prior permission
of the publisher and copyright owner.

Stay safe online. Any website addresses listed in this book are correct at the time
of going to print. However, Farshore is not responsible for content hosted by third
parties. Please be aware that online content can be subject to change and websites
can contain content that is unsuitable for children. We advise that all children are
supervised when using the internet.

This book is produced from independently certified FSC™ paper
to ensure responsible forest management.

For more information visit: www.harpercollins.co.uk/green

Hannah Wilson

Samara Hardy

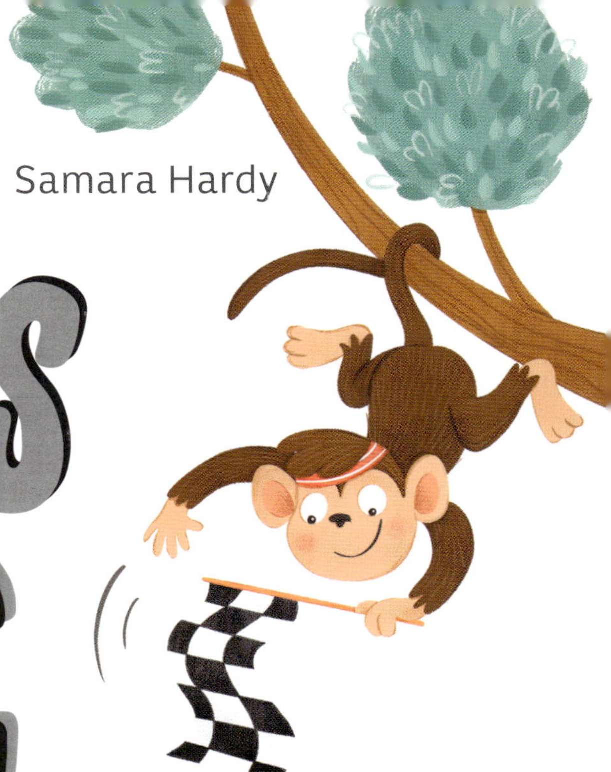

WORRIES BIG AND SMALL WHEN YOU ARE 5

RED SHED

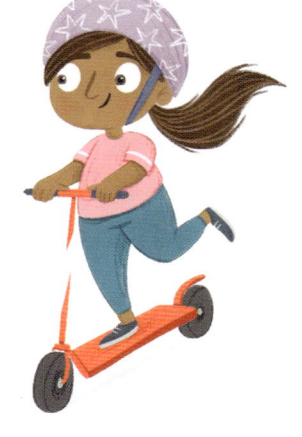

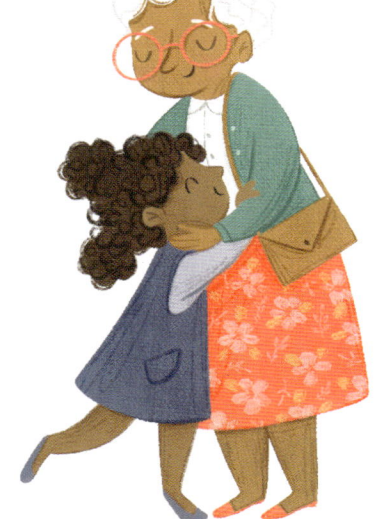

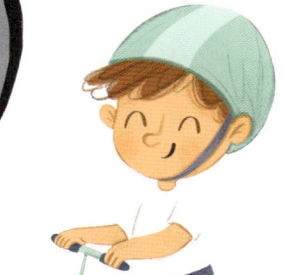

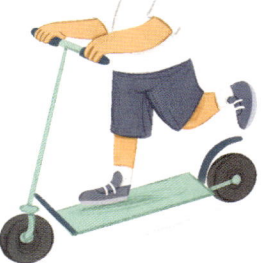

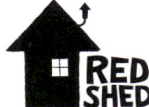

What if . . .

I worry about stuff?	7
I'm feeling sad?	8
I lose my teddy bear?	8
The monster on TV comes to get me?	9
I'm scared of fireworks?	9
A dog runs towards me?	10
I can't find my grown-up?	10
I fall off my scooter?	11
I have to see the dentist?	12
I need a haircut?	12
I'm worried about going to school?	14
No one wants to play with me?	16
I get lost?	16
I get into trouble with the teacher?	17
Someone is mean to me?	17
My friend won't let me play with their toy?	18
My dinner is disgusting?	18
I'm nervous about the dark?	19
There's a thunderstorm?	20
Someone shouts or gets angry?	20
My book has a scary picture?	21
I've drawn on the table?	21
I need a doctor's check-up?	22
The lift breaks down?	24
No one picks me up?	24
I find people in costumes scary?	25
I cut my knee?	25
I get water in my eyes when I swim?	26
I don't make it to the toilet in time?	28
I want someone with me when I go to sleep?	29

What if I worry about stuff?

A worry is an uncomfortable feeling about a situation. Perhaps a feeling of fear during a thunderstorm or of nervousness about seeing the doctor. EVERYBODY worries about stuff. Big stuff, little stuff, all kinds of stuff. You might think some of your worries are silly. They're NOT. All worries are important as they can stop us from doing things.

Worries are a normal part of life. We can't get rid of all of them, but we can stop them bossing us around. The best way to deal with a worry is to TALK ABOUT IT with a grown-up you trust. In this book, I call this person 'your grown-up'. Your grown-up is probably your mum, dad or the person who looks after you — or all three! You can tell your grown-up (or grown-ups) ANYTHING. It can be hard talking about things that worry us, but it's lovely to get a hug and a thank you for being so brave for sharing our feelings. So let's get chatting about tricky stuff and stop worries getting in the way of fun!

WORRIES BOTHER US AT DIFFERENT AGES. IF YOU ARE OLDER OR YOUNGER THAN FIVE, THIS BOOK IS STILL FOR YOU!

What if I'm feeling sad?

Well done for working out that you're sad and for thinking about it. EVERYBODY feels sad from time to time. Sadness is a NORMAL human emotion (feeling), like anger or happiness. But it doesn't feel nice, does it? Do you know what made you sad? Can you and your grown-up make a plan to try to stop it making you sad? Sometimes you just have to be patient and wait for the sadness to fade. While you wait, do something that makes you happy!

What if I lose my teddy bear?

It's horrible to lose any toy, especially your favourite teddy, so it's OK to feel sad. It might help if you can do something useful. MAKE A PLAN to find your teddy. Where can you look? Can anyone help? If you STILL can't find it, imagine teddy on an exciting adventure. Hopefully, teddy will return one day to tell you about it!

What if I'm scared of fireworks?

What worries you? The loud bangs? They can make ANYONE jump! Try pulling a thick hat over your ears or borrow some earmuffs. Remember that a noise can't hurt you. Or do the fiery explosions scare you? They happen VERY far away, so they won't hurt you either.

Or is it the dark or the crowds of people? Describe the worries to your grown-up and chat about ideas to make them smaller. Then, knowing you are SAFE, snuggle up and watch the rockets burst into beautiful colours and sparkles. WOWEE!

What if the monster on TV comes to get me?

Monsters do NOT exist in real life, so that will never happen. Monsters exist only in the imagination of people who make TV shows or write books. If you find a monster hanging out in YOUR imagination, tell it to BUZZ OFF! If it STILL bothers you, put your amazing mind to work. I'm imagining my silly monster wearing spotty pyjamas, swimming in a jelly lake. What can YOU imagine?

What if a dog runs towards me?

Keep calm, still and quiet. If you shout or run away, the dog might think you want to play and chase you. Once the dog has sniffed you, it will probably go away or its owner will come to get it. Most dogs are FRIENDLY FURBALLS, so ask your grown-up and the dog's owner if you ever feel like patting a pooch!

What if I can't find my grown-up?

Before each trip out, plan what to do if you get lost. At the park, could you and your grown-up meet by the swings? Or, often it's best to STAY WHERE YOU ARE and shout your grown-up's name. They will find you soon. If you are waiting a long time, look for a grown-up with children and tell them you need help.

What if I fall off my scooter?

OUCH! Poor you! Take a DEEP BREATH. Then another one. How are you feeling now? When I fall over, I often feel more shocked than hurt. (That can still be scary and make me feel like crying.) If your body DOES hurt, tell your grown-up. If not, get up and get scooting. Don't let one fall stop you having fun!

DON'T WALK OFF WITH ANYONE WHO ISN'T YOUR GROWN-UP.

SHOUT LOUDLY IF A STRANGER BOTHERS YOU.

What if I have to see the dentist?

It's great news that the dentist is going to check if your teeth are healthy. The dentist's room looks a bit like a SPACESHIP — white, shiny and full of cool equipment! See the big padded chair? That's for YOU. Hop on. Comfy, isn't it? Lie back and — this is the fun bit — the chair will tilt backwards and rise up!

CHECK-UPS DO NOT HURT!

What if I need a haircut?

Cutting hair keeps it strong and healthy, but the hairdresser's salon can be a noisy, busy place. Is there anything about it you find tricky? Can you tell your grown-up or the hairdresser? They can help you feel more comfortable. Now let's head to the salon!

First, you'll put on a long cape so you don't get covered in hair. Fancy a hair wash? GREAT! Lean back on the curved sink, close your eyes and enjoy the warm water and sweet smells.

OPEN WIDE! The dentist will look at your teeth, perhaps using a mirror on a stick to see behind them. Are they wearing gloves and a face mask? That stops germs. I bet you brush your teeth twice a day, so they'll be in tip-top condition.

All done! If you're lucky, you'll get to rinse with minty mouthwash. Spit it into the tiny sink next to the chair. And if you're REALLY lucky, you'll get a STICKER!

A quick blast of warm air with the blow-dryer, a dollop of special cream, and you're ready to head home looking SUPER SNAZZY!

Here's the spinning chair! The hairdresser might use a pedal to pump it up, up, up! While they expertly snip away, relax and sit still. The hairdresser may gently tilt your head to cut different parts of your hair. If you want VERY short hair, the clippers might come out. Try not to giggle — they are a little TICKLY!

What if I'm worried about going to school?

School helps you grow up and learn about the world. But it's very different from home, so many children find it a bit tricky. Are you about to go to school for the first time or move to a new school? Or does your usual school just make you feel a little wobbly? Whatever the situation, it should help if we chat about the tricky bits, and look for FUN!

Shall we say good morning to your teacher? I bet we get a "good morning" back! Now, hang up your coat and bag and put away your water bottle. If you don't know where something goes, ASK YOUR TEACHER. They'll look after you and tell you everything you need to know.

What do you think is the trickiest bit about school? For many children, it's saying goodbye to their grown-up. Give them a BIG HUG. Can you make them giggle? How about saying, "See you later, alligator!" (It's nice to think about seeing them later.) You're going to be SO BUSY that you probably won't miss your grown-up too much.

What can you see in the classroom? Toys, books, games? CHILDREN? If you don't know them, tell them your name and find out theirs. You'll soon make some new friends. Are you getting hungry? GOOD NEWS: It's snack time soon! Then the teacher will take everyone outside for a play. YIPPEE!

Listen to your teacher! If you need help, just ask!

After lunch, your teacher knows you'll be tired. So sit on the carpet, have a sneaky yawn and listen to a story. Then it's home time. Home time is HUG TIME with your grown-up! Tell them all about your exciting day. They'll be SO proud of you. But how do YOU feel?

What if no one wants to play with me?

How do you feel about this? It's difficult, isn't it? But I think if you do some playground investigation, you'll find there ARE children to play with. Is anyone kicking a ball or playing catch? Who's got toys out? Ask if you can play or just join in.

If they say you CAN'T, they're just being grumpy. Find someone else to play with — or start your OWN game. Others might want to join YOU. If you still feel a bit funny (many kids do), tell your teacher. They'll have some ideas to make playtime more peachy.

What if I get lost?

We all get lost sometimes, especially in big busy places like schools. Your school is full of grown-ups who will look after you and keep you safe. So what should you do if you get lost? Yup, find a grown-up! They will probably ask you for your class or teacher's name, or your name. They'll take you back to your classroom or point you in the right direction. NO PROBLEM!

What if I get into trouble with the teacher?

ALL children get told off by a teacher at some time or another. It doesn't feel nice, but the teacher needs to tell you if you did something wrong. So you can try not to do it again. Do you know WHY you did what you did? How were you feeling at the time? Bored, annoyed, confused, tired? Tell your teacher. They want to hear how you are, so they can help you BEFORE there is a problem.

What if someone is mean to me?

When someone does or says something unkind, it's usually because they're grumpy, sad or upset. They don't really mean it. But it still feels horrible. So let's work out what to do. Tell the meanie, "You are not being very kind." If they are still mean, WALK AWAY or IGNORE THEM. Try not to be mean back. You'll feel so proud if you stay kind, calm and AS COOL AS A CUCUMBER. If someone is mean often – or hurts you – tell a grown-up.

What if my friend won't let me play with their toy?

Ask them politely if you could have a little play with the toy when they have finished with it. Try suggesting a SWAP. Can you lend a toy to your friend? If they still say no, NEVERMIND. You can't make someone do something. You can only control YOUR OWN actions. If YOU always share your toys, maybe your friend will learn to share soon. Can you tell them WHY you think sharing is important and fun?

What if my dinner is disgusting?

I bet it's not THAT disgusting! Let's try it again. How does the food FEEL? Soft or crunchy, creamy or chewy? Can you guess all the ingredients? Your body needs different foods to grow healthily, so be a FOOD EXPLORER. The more you try different stuff, the more you will learn to like it. Those tiny green trees (broccoli!) might taste DELICIOUS one day soon!

What if I'm nervous about the dark?

Imagine a ball turning around next to your bedside lamp. That's like our planet, Earth, slowly spinning next to the Sun. The lit side facing the lamp (or Sun) is daytime. The other side is dark night. So night is the SAME as day, but with no light from the Sun.

Can you think of some nice things about the dark? I like to think about how the inky night sky helps us to see the beautiful shining moon and twinkling stars.

Darkness also tells our brain that it's time to rest. So the dark will help you to sleep better. Can you imagine darkness as a blanket, snuggling you down for the night? And if you ever need help relaxing, try a BELLY BALLOON. Lie on your back and rest your hand on your tummy. Breathe slowly in and out, feeling your belly inflate and deflate like a balloon.

What if there's a thunderstorm?

Thunder means exciting things are happening in the sky, and you might get a free light show! Those claps and rumbles are caused by LIGHTNING – a bright flash of electricity. The lightning heats the air, which BOOMS as it suddenly gets bigger. Light travels more quickly than sound, so you will probably SEE the lightning before you HEAR the thunder.

Count the seconds between the lightning and thunder. Every three seconds means you are one kilometre from the storm.

What if someone shouts or gets angry?

It can be quite a shock when someone shouts, gets angry or says a bad word. Especially if that someone is a grown-up. But people aren't perfect, and everyone can get upset now and again. Tiptoe away and give them some space and time to calm down. THEY should worry about their actions, not you.

What if my book has a scary picture?

Look at the picture with your grown-up and chat about what you find scary. Does it show something real? If it's a dragon, relax – they are FICTIONAL. They don't exist in real life. PHEW!

If it's a REAL photograph, perhaps of a tiger or snake, BE BRAVE and look at it closely. Talk about how those claws or scales help these wonderful animals find food and move about. Facts will help your fears fade away.
If the picture is STILL scary, it's OK not to look at it.

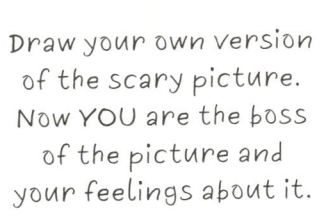

Draw your own version of the scary picture. Now YOU are the boss of the picture and your feelings about it.

What if I've drawn on the table?

Even if it was an accident, tell a grown-up straightaway, SAY SORRY and help clean up. The grown-up might be cross. Try to understand why – perhaps the table is new and your drawing of a baboon's bottom is hard to wipe away! But they won't be cross for long and they'll be pleased that you told them about your mistake and said sorry.

What if I need a doctor's check-up?

Everybody needs to see the doctor from time to time, and a check-up is a great way to make sure your body is growing healthily. Your visit will be quick and simple. If the doctor thinks medicine or treatment might be helpful, they'll let your grown-up know.

Right, let's find out what a doctor's job is all about and check out some VERY COOL GADGETS!

First, step onto the SCALES to measure your weight. Then stand next to a wallchart or measuring stick to see how tall you are.

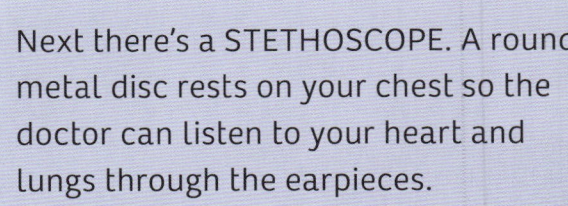

YOUR EYESIGHT MIGHT BE TESTED WITH A LETTER CHART!

Next there's a STETHOSCOPE. A round metal disc rests on your chest so the doctor can listen to your heart and lungs through the earpieces.

An OTOSCOPE has a magnifying glass and a light to help the doctor look inside your ears.

LOLLIPOP time! (Just the stick, I'm afraid.) The stick gently presses down your tongue so the doctor can see inside your throat. They might use a PENLIGHT – a pen that's also a torch. (Yes, I want one too!)

Don't panic if the doctor gets out a HAMMER! It's made of rubber and won't hurt at all. The doctor will gently tap your knees and – here's the SUPERCOOL bit – your legs will kick out all by themselves! That's called a reflex.

A THERMOMETER measures body temperature. It might scan your forehead or sit gently in your ear.

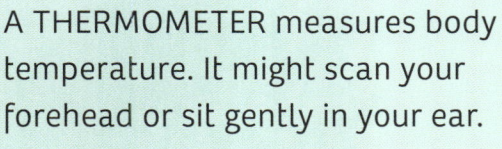

All finished. Thank you, doctor! Now you can go home and give your TEDDIES a health check.

What if the lift breaks down?

Most machines break down every now and then and need to be repaired. If the lift stops working, a grown-up will press a button to tell the lift manager. Someone will come very soon to restart the lift from the outside. EASY PEASY. While you wait, how about playing Rock, Paper, Scissors? Or having a good old singsong?

What if no one picks me up?

You have NOT been forgotten. Your grown-up is just a little late – perhaps they got delayed at the shops or the dog ate the car keys (AGAIN!). Someone will call them and find out how long they'll be. At school, you can wait in the classroom or office. What useful or fun activities will pass the time?

What if I find people in costumes scary?

Are you thinking about HALLOWEEN costumes? They can frighten anyone! But the only thing REAL about those witches, skeletons and vampires is the person underneath, wanting to take off that itchy mask or sweaty suit.

Or is it the big furry bear costume you saw in town? Those suits are HUGE and it is weird not seeing who's inside. But watch for a bit — you might find you're brave enough to give that bear a wave. You'll feel proud of your new confidence.

What if I cut my knee?

It may hurt for a bit, but you'll soon feel better. A grown-up might clean the cut and use an antiseptic cream to keep out germs. You may not need a plaster — your body can make its own one. A SCAB is a hard layer that protects a cut as it heals. DON'T PICK IT! The scab will slowly shrink until your skin is as good as new. Great job, body!

What if I get water in my eyes when I swim?

You'll probably get water EVERYWHERE! The water won't hurt you, but it can feel uncomfortable if it gets in your eyes. Don't rub them. BLINK SLOWLY three times to get rid of the water.

Have you tried goggles? They really help — and they'll show you an AMAZING UNDERWATER WORLD. Practise putting your head underwater, with or without goggles. Do this in stages. (YOU decide the stages.)

Could stage one be holding your breath above the water? Stage two might be dipping just your chin under the water. It won't be long until you can sink your whole head under like a submarine!

What if I don't make it to the toilet in time?

Have a wee BEFORE you go out, as it's harder to find a toilet when you're out and about. (Your grown-up will find one, though.) Tell them before you REALLY need a wee or a poo, so you don't have to run to the loo like a cheetah on sport's day!

If you DO accidentally wet or poop your pants, there's no need to feel bad. It's a soggy situation, but it happens to EVERYONE when they're young. Your grown-up will clean you up and find some dry clothes. You'll soon feel comfortable again.

What if I want someone with me when I go to sleep?

Your mum, dad or grown-up love you SO much. But it's hard for them to stay with you as you fall asleep. They need some time to do jobs or relax. They want you to get used to going to sleep on your own. It's a normal part of growing up, but it can feel a little tricky. What feels tricky for you?

Is it the dark? Read about darkness on p.19, and leave your door open a little wider. Or is it being on your own? You're not REALLY on your own. Your grown-up is nearby. Can you hear them pottering about? And snuggling with your teddies, you're DEFINITELY not on your own. So close your eyes and make pictures with your mind. How about a towering, golden sandcastle? Good night!